HELIX

Helix

NEW AND SELECTED POEMS

John Steffler

SIGNAL EDITIONS IS AN IMPRINT OF VÉHICULE PRESS

Published with the generous assistance of The Canada Council for the Arts and the Book Publishing Industry Development Program of the Department of Canadian Heritage.

The poems that originally appeared in *That Night We Were Ravenous* are used with the permission of McClelland & Stewart. The poems that originally appeared in *The Grey Islands* are used with the permission of Brick Books.

Signal Editions editor: Carmine Starnino
Cover design: David Drummond
Photograph of the author: Susan Gillis
Set in Minion by Simon Garamond
Special assistance: Rosemary Dardick
Printed by AGMV-Marquis Inc.

CANADIAN CATALOGUING IN PUBLICATION DATA

Steffler, John, 1947-
Helix : new and selected poems / John Steffler.

ISBN 1-55065-160-9

I. Title.

PS8587.T346H45 2002   C811'.54   C2002-904975-X
PR9199.3.S7814H45 2002

Published by Véhicule Press, Montréal, Québec, Canada
www.vehiculepress.com

Distribution in Canada by LPG Distribution
orders@lpg.ca

Distributed in the U.S. by Independent Publishers Group
www.ipgbook.com

Printed and bound in Canada.

Contents

THAT NIGHT WE WERE RAVENOUS

For Susan

Wreckage of Play

SAINT LAURENCE'S TEARS

No questions of falling then,
the August earth of Ontario under our backs—summer's
whole history we floated our small witnessing lives upon—
my sister and I in the star-showering night,
counting the quick silver scores
like lightning the crickets made
when their white-hot music built too intricate-tall
and fell, starting again.

No question of sinking
safe on the land that wanted us,
ocean of loam so many had sailed their houses on,
its slow cooperative swell thick with all it had borne,
gathered back: flints, coins, kitchen knives
in shallow constellations below,

the farm's old owners still setting
their lanterns down at the mouth of a stall,

harness riding into the strength it borrowed from.

LABRADOR ROAD

You go through your lifetime's allotment of hiccups
on fast forward,
driving this Labrador road

with alders and black spruce on the blurred
margins and sometimes canyons of snow,

your face jiggling loose, eyeholes out of line,
fingers bunched wrong in their large skins,

until you'd swear you're flying some
set of drums, the dashboard lights
a miniature city below.

Only car on the Esker road
in western Labrador, a fifteen-pound trout
gutted and stiffening in the trunk, you gargle:
in the pines, in the pines
where the sun never shines...

white moon rising, big as the face of your
mother over your crib, really another
country you could sail to,
more rock floating alongside.

HOLLIS STREET SQUARE, HALIFAX

Two kinds in the Saturday crowd:
first, the sharp-edged uneroded ones, single
or in fresh pairs, click by
briskly on assertive heels. Themselves
what they offer the world, a craft-fair of faces.

And then those with children at the ends
of their arms, small versions of themselves brightly
inflating as they drain down,
as though they'd opened a vein in their wrists and
out poured blood taking the shape of a child
pulling them by the hand:

those getting brighter and brisker and those
going invisible, sucked up the straws
of six-year-old arms, diving
inside small skins,
starting over again, small.

VACATION

looked at plainly
the word itself states the whole point:
not surf and bikinis and terrace cafes
      but vacancy
      evacuation

you break a hole in the business of your life,
disappear,
your room deserted, sealed up,
the places you work, paths you bustle along
               are without you

and outside the circuitry of routine
you too are vacant, a happy "o" the world
flows in and out of

               down rippling fields, sky-
swallowed figures, dust-yellow, pitching hay;
crowds in the cavernous shout, surging across at the lights;
the rivers, the horns and graves pour shining and weeping
into you and you hold them

               and let go,
you have nowhere to keep them so far from home

and each morning, waking, for one sky-wide
moment, unborn again, you are purely
the world

        you do not know who or where
          you are

TOWERS AND MONUMENTS

three hundred years
and what's there to show?

earthquakes are not the problem, but the sea
always quakes more than the earth ever has
and we live on its edge

balancing
boats on the waves
homes on the shrugging rock

the framing we build spans shore and grey horizon
every day, but the sea slides after us
erasing what we've done

the towers, the monuments you miss are *there*
in the space between ocean and heaven,
we trace them, conjure them out of bustling air
in our songs and stories, we hold them
wild again on the crest of the running instant
and let them go,
back to our dead and the faint days

with nothing to show

BOILER ROOM MEN

Boiler room men in their nests
of machinery under the underground parking lots, behind
steel doors, are all comfortable
cowards, wise *philosophes*

who slapped the gym mat frantically long ago in some
watershed wrestling match with the drafty
tumbledown world—and women what they are, clacking
around in their high heels overhead—gave up trying to
build some weather-tight enterprise of their own,
oh better,

much better to serve the big boys' corporate physical plant
like eunuch slaves at the emperor's bed,
maintaining the apparatus of power
from time to time,
their stocking feet propped otherwise on a steam pipe, the
hockey game yelping away on a small TV.

Even room for a cat down here
or at least a kettle for tea.

For Christ sake, who needs high pay

in a place as safe as this,
even taking into account the risk of explosion
which is kind of neat?

And it's as good as having money in the bank or jeans
the ladies can't take their eyes off, watching
the needle dials tremble, holding
the kilo-pascals, the obedient power that's really
all theirs,
that they didn't have to raise.

MONSTER BAIT

Hovering near me, contorted with chortles
and shrill challenges, his feet already running
in several directions,
my two-year-old son is being irresistible
monster bait.

For the seventh time, I roar
after him, slap my shoes an inch from his blurring heels,
slavering, Lon Chaney's look-alike,

but this time,
when he turns at bay by his bed, squealing, quivering,
and I lumber forward to make the kill,
I've gone too far.

At the sight of my face, so willfully twisted,
he bolts into tears, and I
instantly am my own father, struck
by the strange inevitability:

son-scaring
son-comforting now
having known the small part so well
and knowing I looked precisely as my father had
in our games, when the magic became too strong
and I broke, seeing him change,
desert me so easily

to let a stranger look through his eyes.

WHAT THE EARTH DREAMT AND DID

Side by side in bed
listening to the rain surge and fade
and surge across the roof in cold pelleting,
it seemed a black sea lashed in blackness had swallowed
the countryside, and our house alone
like a small boat
pitched and rode out the storm.

But here in the young light
the only traces of what the earth dreamt and did
are the shovel freshly blossoming rust
and the garden wheelbarrow
a bird is bathing in.

IN THE TENT OF MY MIDNIGHT LAMP

In the tent of my midnight lamp
I am bent to a poem.

Thoughts branch out and out on mountain plateau roads,
Incan cobbles,
dueling with animals and saints
that are the same.

My son calls.
The poem breaks.
I go in the dark to his small bed, his legs
like speared otters, twisting with pain.

My poem has snapped like a dry stick.
I sit in the spring-green, child-breathed
air, humming,
blessed to be holding muscle and bone,
urging such new limbs to grow.

THE NEW SLED

The new sled
which the boy insists on calling
the GT Snowracer
and is no mere sled in his opinion
(the very word sled makes him laugh with brief
contempt as he pulls his woolen helmet on)
can swoop like an osprey
down the valley's white throat

can veer out of sight in the afternoon
which is only sky

and the boy, from a far speck,
against regrettable gravity, comes
wrestling his hawk-hearted companion back
to the father-held earth,
flame-faced and loud with something of what a hawk
must know.

BITS OF MOSS

good thing, a little decay and wear—
not *memento mori* exactly—but it hugs
us into the process,
the movement

the wood my table is made of
I like best here where some guy yanked
nails out years ago, splinters
flying, and it still had time to smooth
and grey before I got hold of it

things melting, crumbling, settling down, molecular
bits leaping off sharp corners, the shiny
slides, like divers—*yippeee*! here I come!—out into space

and the young things
crisp bright tender thingumajigs shooting
up through the rubble, noisy and keen—look at us!—
new champions everywhere

it suits me
seeing this
seeing myself slow down
the bald patches, bits of moss here and there,
being half sunk in the ground helps
solve a lot of things

US PLUMBERS

we're like surgeons,
that's what people don't realize,
a bad pipe in there,
something blocked or dripping
and we got to cut in and find it.

they think it's all monkey-wrench work,
but shovel and saw, I say,
shovel and saw are my most important tools,
you got to dig right in and not be fussy how you do it
or what you go through,
walls swollen with bad water—like slicing
a boil—down through concrete sometimes
a couple of feet thick or flower-beds with people
hopping around, watch out for that rose! dig out the bulbs
first, won't you?
hell, it's like asking a surgeon to take out the moles before
he goes after a blood clot,
you got to dig fast, wood, plaster, ground, whatever, all
just junk in the way, you kick it aside, you learn
to see *pipes* inside,
everything else invisible,
go for them like a diver in water, just get your
hands on those pipes, everything flowing, on to the next
job, new leaks and jams every second,
let whatever you dig through heal itself.

other people help it along.

MY LATEST INVENTION

I'm working on something even better than
the neutron bomb:
a device that destroys everything
but people
and plumbing.

Can't you see it!
Above the traffic and high-rise apartments
a flash, a soft
thump.
People strolling in the streets blink
and look around at this jungle
of monkey bars.

Folks floating in their tubs
are suddenly surrounded by nothing
but blue.

On toilets, hundreds of feet in the air
people sit tight
and stare across at one another
like astonished robins.

The bulky dross of building material
has vanished,
revealing the undreamt of beauty, the plumber's art:
breathtaking trees of naked pipes soaring and branching to
bathtubs, sinks and urinals, all hanging in air
like porcelain fruit.

Alexander Calder's heart would burst!

Of course there *will* be casualties.

A lot of people will fall.
Only those at ground level
or on the john or in the tub
and maybe a few who are shaving or brushing their teeth
and manage to grab the sink when the floor disappears
will be saved.

But then, no weapon is perfect,
and my plumbing bomb at least
has the advantage of favouring
clean people.

dripping tap.
I figure: 15 minutes,
the usual thing, work it in on the way somewhere
else. like paying a social call, washer, wrench and stuff
in my pocket. feeling light, empty-handed. almost
silly to charge for it.

but Jesus, look at the place.
stone gate. big trees. around a bend
this huge glass house. sun pouring through it like a prism.
glass roof curving to long eaves.
glass brick walls.
foundation the same, the guy said later.
(part of the Corning family. ones with the glass factory
in the States. lunatic fringe I guess. lost in money.)
house of the future he said.
never wear out, never need paint.
even the door was thick glass
etched with birds and plants.

a woman opened it without a stitch on
(I've seen *that* before, but this one
acted as though she was dressed),
said take off your clothes, come right in and don't
bring anything in that's not made of glass.

Neil and I sat in the van.

she answered the door again. I said lady
the clothes are no problem, but a glass
wrench?
her husband comes up (bare-ass too) says
what's the trouble?

as if we're the crazy ones O.K.! O.K.! I said,
let's take a look at the thing!

even Neil's ring had to stay behind.
I laughed—hey Neil you look like a shaved bear with its
hair coming back!
Mr. and Mrs. never cracking a smile.
us fat. white. beside them brown and bony.
even their furniture was glass.
and the plumbing!
you could see glass pipes in the walls,
bubbles zipping up risers, clear glass tub. the works.
you could sit in the dining room, watch
somebody taking a bath overhead!

yep she's leaking alright I said, you
wouldn't happen to have a glass screwdriver and wrench?
screwdriver, yes, he says. he got that far himself.
but glass wrench? no.
what the hell did you call me for? I asked
standing there stark naked
you expect me to have a Jesus glass wrench?

he said he thought perhaps
the rest of the world
was becoming a little more enlightened
in its attitude toward glass.

for all I know their tap's still dripping.

the kind that's gold-plated is *nothing*. they've got them in the Sears catalogue.

but handmade ones, no two the same, order them up special, artist's signature carved on each! that sort of thing. ones like animal heads cut from fancy stone, rubber ones like parts of the body I don't need to name—very lifelike too, by Jesus (those roped off with a warning sign)—you should've *seen* the crowds—more kinds of taps than you'd dream up in a whole year!

and nothing *but* taps! acres of them! and signs in eleven languages: the world's first exposition devoted strictly to taps.

ones with dials for just the right volume and pressure and spray type and temperature, the water coloured or perfumed, and taps with real long thin spouts going way up and around and around, and real old ones like the Romans had, and computer ones that come on at a certain time, and ones that come on when you talk to them, no kidding, just stand there and say "warm please" or "cold" and out she comes, great for the guy with no hands when he wants to wash up before supper, and fine solid brass ones like you don't see anymore— Neil and I must've handled those for an hour. that was the one address I took down, place in England. lost it later in a bar.

and the noise and handshakes and elbows and lights everywhere, real bright light jumping off millions of taps, chrome and nickel and glass, ones for dams as big as a bloody house, others the size of mosquitoes, rows and rows of them till it actually hurt your eyes.

Jesus I dreamt taps for weeks.

FIRST MEMORIES

oakum.
stiff sugary hair, tarry
and sweet when the hot lead hits it.

cinnamon hair.

blowtorch roars on its back,
blue fire talons gripping the iron cup.

my grandfather's gloved hands
tipping the bright lead,
bright rivers.

around us shadows jostle the stone walls
the webby joists
ghosting us close and important,
silent in work
and the lantern's glow.

FROM HALKI

Along a lane through olive fields
with Mount Zas close in the brilliant air
and no sound but birds and the bamboo's watery
rustle, we come to a chapel and burying ground
in a pine's dry shade. One small flame

in the chapel's gloom and Saint George killing his dragon
forever. This chamber deep in the local mind,
out here open to all, makes the rest of the land
seem like the rest of the mind. Outside the graveyard
wall I pick up a broken cross carved

with name and dates, and the littered earth focuses,
strikes like a snake, the yellow sticks cracking
under my shoes are thigh bones, ribs still
tangled in black rags. The brightness, the branches
swoop with the bones in a blurred stream up

through my legs, out of my mouth and eyes and down
again in magnetic curves. Nothing is hidden
here, made abstract. No one pretends this walled
ground is a resting place; only a dark
hall each passes slowly through traveling

back. And walking again I see the tawny earth
everywhere is brick, pottery, tools, teeth,
dung, things built and broken, grown
and eaten over and over, burnt to fine
ash in the young Aegean sun.

AFTERNOON: MONI

Stairway streets, white
beyond corporeality, the small square
shuttered, holding only the steep light, the Achaean
wind shuffling cornered leaves as it always has,
striding from island to island.

Birds in a gust,
a glitter of olive hills. In the plains
the windmills creak on their empty boles. The unobserved
world moves without the impatience of men—laid
in prisms of sleep at the height of the day—

that time might return to its infancy,
that the gods might value the earth in privacy

and give it touched by their fabulous passions
back to men.

THE SAME DISCOVERY

for Jane Rabnett

Six hundred years ago, the clay-roofed
town under his coat's flapping skirt
(the same blue distance north to Mykonos,
the painted boats trembling in liquid sky),
a newly landed steward of Marco Sanudo,
pausing here for the castle hill's view,
found a vein of eternity far from San Marco Square
and never left, but had his heart's discovery
framed in these walls, their deep-set windows
holding what he had seen that August afternoon;

so that entering your house, this room's
view of boats and buildings hanging in blue space,
we enter the same discovery, finding
a home we already know, borderless
time with its seasons and eloquent winds,
stretching at last to our full unfearful size.

The Grey Islands

◆

driving all day. mist and rain. the highway
deserted. miles of bunchbacked spruce. grey sea
butting the rock.

along the mud road to Roddickton. dark backwoods
feeling. bush on all sides. gravel pits. old
machines along the way.

hardly a soul.

◆

This man waiting there! The thing I can't get out of my
mind. The last thing Leonard mentioned. Practically tossed
it in the window as I drove off, like it hardly mattered at all.
A madman is living alone out there. The one inhabitant left.
Holding out in the ruined town. Holding the whole island in
his head. Thinking it into reality, every stick, every bird.
And god knows what else. What will he do when I step into
his thoughts?

◆

All that tension the past month. Days gone by in a blur. The trouble with breaking attachments, ending routines.

The council boys cautiously nodding, "Sure. Okay. A leave of absence if you want." Patey of course: "Are you sure we shouldn't be looking for a new town planner?" And I tell them again I'll let them know in September, I just need time off. And their eyes shift away. But they're good enough to wish me luck.

With Karen it's a different thing. She knows why I'm doing this, approves even, sees signs of life in my decision. And summer in Ontario is a dream for her, the stores and films, days at the lake. And in a way she's just as glad to go without me, my restlessness a bother to her when we're there. But still. A whole summer apart. Both of us wondering is this how the end begins? And she's annoyed because it's my initiative, and she's left to react, do what she has to because of me. Stuck with the kids. While I'm off indulging in masculine idleness, chasing a selfish whim. As soon as I mentioned it she started guarding herself, taking charge of her fatherless brood like I was just visiting. Tough, going back to her family alone though. All of them so alert to the smell of divorce. Quick with contingency plans, personal strategies. They'll take her into their arms, drooling condolences, and she'll have to say over and over, "It's not like that!" Hating my guts.

◆

Parsons Pond. Low buildings. Take-outs, confectioneries
hiked up on stilts next to the shoulder. Girls on the highway
three abreast, eating plates of chips. Two-hundred pounders.
Sausaged into their jeans. I wave and give them a wide berth.
People always strolling right on the pavement here. Bored
and playing chicken with the passing cars. Hunting bold
proposals, long rides. And why should cars have the only
pavement to themselves? All the rest of the place puddles,
potholes and broken rock. And the road is where people have
always walked. A guy in a car no more important than
someone in rubber boots. I like this. Blocking the highway
while you chat with a few friends.

◆

hunting country.
hills and ponds poker-faced,
guarded.

close to the road, small
quick-built homes, pickups, skidoos
parked among trees. people
live light
able to strike fast at

things that are passing by:
animals, birds, fish, work,
money in any form.

◆

down the last hill and
it's Englee.
good junky bustle.
rocks and houses tossed together. gulls
and rigging. boats docked among roofs it looks.
planks crossing ditches to candy shacks. Hostess
Coke Rothmans signs trailing down their
fronts like medals, honourary
membership in that world.

I park, spattered pickups all around,
and walk the muddy harbour lane.
stages, wharves, woodpiles, sheds
patched propped tilting grey clamber over the water.
sunk cars waving kelp, boats rotting keel up,
chickens, nets, rusting drums.

houses back up tight to the cliff.

every window curtain shifts.
pale hands, faces rise
from crocheted shadows.

kids walk by say hello. turn. walk by again. hello
pass again for another look.

one guy in back of his pickets chopping wood.
I say hello. he bends, his hands in the chips,
watches me under his arm.

◆

At the airport though in that last white minute under the
lights, it was good, it was stronger than ever between us. No
trace of desertion or revenge. That date in September, that
goal, all of us coming home, the strongest thing in our lives.
The frame for everything else.

Lifting Peter and Anna, feeling their slender arms was the
hardest thing, knowing I'll find them older and grown when I
touch them again. To miss so much of their lives.

◆

he's out there the kids say pointing.
a little hut. the far end of a loose beaver dam.
Nels's stage.
must be so familiar to him and his family
they don't even see it anymore,
run, scramble sure-footed over the holes
and wobbles.

to me it's a jungle.
trip-vines, man-traps, where do you put your feet
for godsake, gaps, loose sticks teeter-totter,
water right under you.
hello!
I poke my head in the low door, rafters
dangling every kind of gaff and rusty implement.
an old man at the splitting table.
two boys perch watching him sharpen
squid jiggers with a file.

he shakes my hand, cautious,
feeling what kind of man.
traveller. landsman.
(salesman? missionary? taxman? crook?)
I want to get to the island I tell him,
hear he takes people out.

he spits. goes back to filing.

it spiles a day, he warns.

then flings out what it'll cost.
if we can go on the water.

I wait.

am I with the government?
no no! I'm (what'll I call myself?)

I just want to spend some time out there.
fish for trout

he cuts his price in half

◆

Nels and his wife and half a dozen or so of their kids are loading empty barrels into a boat. "Goin squiddin," Nels says.

I ask if there's room for me.

"Y'ever done it before?"

"Nope."

"It's terrible dirty work," he warns, his eyes bright with glee.

I tell him that's okay, and he sends his youngest boy to find me a pair of rubber trousers.

I step into them, pull the braces up and grab a barrel to take aboard.

They do me the favour of letting me try to help.

Later Nels moves the barrel to where it was meant to be.

they all save one last squirt
till they're clear of the water,
black splats straight in the air,
up your sleeve, into your eye.

we sit tossing our jiggers,
ducking, chuckling, piling up squids
easy as pie.

"Take a chunk outa ya big as a dime,"
Nels says, shaking one down that's
braided around his arm.

"Fall in there and they'd drown ya,
drag ya down."

dark in the water long forms shoot criss-cross
like limbs of a sunken forest. strange.
not the same things we're pulling in,
stringy legs, flabby pouches.

coming up they ink wildly, puff like
parachutes. trying to put on the brakes.

dying they make small sunsets
with their bodies. glow blood-orange, freckle
like trout, huff, sigh. drain iridescent
green. lemon. white.

"Dry 'em on a line," Nels says. "Wintertime,
put 'em in a toaster same as a slice a bread.
Sure! Better 'n potato chips!"

◆

to Nels and his family,
going to live alone on an island is madness,
terrifying to contemplate.

I can see a shrinking point in their eyes
when they ask me: "Won't ya get lonely out there?"
they know these islands, stories of people
lost, stranded, gone mad.
I answer, "No."
and then, "At least I don't *think* I will."
since it's a tricky question with me too
and as much as I'd like to put them at ease
show that I'm no hare-brained mainlander
off to blithely feed himself to the sea,
I don't want to boast. because
I don't know what the night and the island spirits
will do to me.
and more than anything else
I'm afraid of pride.

◆

scoured sky. wind
and open miles.
all morning we climb the bright
hills cresting across our course,
pitching us up, sledding us sideways
down, wallowing, walled in water.
                    quick. near us
and gone,
            slim birds flit low, banking,
twisting, skimming the closing troughs,
and I feel it,
                know it a laughing
fact: the harder your hungry eyes bite
into the world (the island cliffs penciled
in blue haze, and *there*, Nels pointing:
whale spray!
                    huge flukes kicking at the sun), the more
you spread your arms to hug it in,
the less you mind the thought of diving under,

eyes flooded. gulping dark.

◆

cliffs
and a thin green
cover. like
dinosaurs crouching under a rug. then

through the rowdy narrows
a sunlit bay: spits, shoals and islands, white
birds lifting out of the blue. no

centre. no shadows here. no lines
leading anywhere. waves
capes scrub-tufts shift, shuffle

under the open sky.

◆

Two rock paws. Between them a gravel beach, a wharf,
the cabin crouched ten feet from the shore. A white
door and a stoop facing the waves. Long grass ducking,
galloping up a hill.

A thick pitted padlock is held to the door with spikes.
Splinters and holes up and down where it's been ripped out
and hammered back. A contest. Keepers and takers. Owners
and travellers. Out here the law is the other way. The right
to shelter takes first place.

Stove, table, two metal bunks. Mattresses once used in
bayonet practice probably. Yellow linoleum nailed to the
table top, dirt deep in the cracks and gashes. Chain oil,
blood, rust, fat, scrawled in like a diary. All the guys gutting
their ducks and fish here, cleaning their guns, stripping their
engines down, hands dripping black spreading bolts and
bearings among the plates of beans.

Feathers turn and lift in the corners when you walk. Back of
the stove mush-bottomed boxes, plastic bags bloated with
rot, shrunk potatoes gone into sprouts, liquid carrots,
cabbages yellow, burst.

Men coming here at the end of their calculations and budgets
and fights and fantasies. Building into crude space. A good
time hacking and arsing out at the furthest edge. No home.
No sofas. No wives. High boots, hunting knives and booze
and not getting washed. Then, the time used up or unable to
stand it another day, laughing and boasting they run to their
boats or planes, dropping what nobody owns. And half what
they brought. Cupboard crammed with stale pancake mix,
margarine, sugar, salt. Salt for godsake! Like me everybody
brings salt. Nobody takes it away.

◆

I thought I was headed for silence
but this island blares and bustles
as hard as any town

the sea slops and thumps
gurgles and knocks
suddenly loud
        (so close I turn expecting some
            person or creature climbing the bank)
suddenly muffled
steered away by the wind rustling
the grass, whispering up the wall

and the gulls
their single distant cries piercing
the shore's roar
their spiral bickering, jeers,
griefs, alarms
sharpen the air: salt
made audible.

even a bumble bee
touring slowly in at the door
and out
can make the cabin hum like a guitar.

◆

For the past two days a longliner has been anchored out in the bay. A cloud of gulls twisting over it shows when the men are gutting their catch. After dark they run a generator and have a light on deck. The sound of the generator stops and the light goes out at about 9:30 or 10:00.

Every once in a while during the day I hear the sudden whine of their speedboat or the deeper beat of their skiff's engine, and I can't help myself: I go to the window or drop what I'm doing to look their way, thinking they might be coming here. But they never are. They zip up the bay somewhere else or out into open water.

When I first got here, I was afraid I'd never be left alone, that having the island's only wharf out front and a spring up behind would mean I'd be on the main track of everyone passing through this part of the world, and that there'd always be people camped around or wanting to share the cabin. But since the first day, I haven't seen a soul.

It's as though everyone cleared out or pulled back the minute I arrived. Whether they did this out of considerateness or shyness or hostility is hard to tell.

◆

black spongy paths,
caribou trails, cut
deep in the wiry scrub,
wander up on the island's plateau,
fade on the rock outcrops

pick up again in the brush,
drop, skirting bogs,
fan into squishy hoof-holes
black soup
stranding you hopping tussock to tussock

then gather again with the rising ground,
thin tracks cleaving mounded moss,
juniper, blueberries, crowberries, heath,
knee-high billions of matted micro-leaves
sharp in blue light tiny fruit trembling

◆

The unfamiliarity of the sounds of the sea combined with the fact that I'm alone here and always half expecting someone to come to the cabin makes me uneasy at night and keeps me from sleeping. An apartment above a busy street would be no worse. I expected the sea to lull me, not keep me awake.

I hear the sound in too much detail. Whole groups and tiers and ranges of sound within and behind the obvious slap and slosh, wash, thump, gurgle and slurp. I hear knocks and hisses and crackles. At times last night it sounded as though the cabin was being hit by a stream of tiny weightless particles—powdered sand in the wind or pellets of snow. I thought it could almost be the sound of fire starting, and got out of bed to look around.

♦

looking south
the Horse Islands floating in blue haze
I stand on rocks scratched
and etched over by ice and wind

littered with glittering silicate chips

patched and padded with small-leaved plants
crabbed things
dry. snaking.
wadded together in knots and tuffets
black wiry hair
white crumbling lumps
claws. crisp bristling spines

everything half bone
half powdered rock

◆

Under everything I'm often vaguely anxious, uneasy in the middle of my actions here. So many things strange to me. The tide for example. It constantly changes the terrain in the low shoreland east of the cabin, and I'm always a bit afraid of getting stranded there.

Paths appear and become submerged. Little knolls that I cross on foot at one time of the day and fix in my memory as landmarks, at another time of the day have turned to islands.

At low tide the sea is bordered by natural meadows. The incoming tide slides up into these grassy fields—a beautiful lush sight—but tricky as far as walking is concerned. It's often impossible to know before stepping forward into the tall grass whether my foot will find solid earth or water below the leaves—and if there is water, how deep it will be.

◆

when the rain comes and a cold wind
with it, it takes me by surprise:
no wood in the cabin. nothing to burn. but
I should have thought of this!
sunshine being the exception here.

I crouch shivering in front of the rusty
stove, trying the doors and vents,
not even sure if it's safe to use.

along the landwash some scattered
sticks, not too deeply soaked,
I split them, get them to burn
and then the real work starts:

braced against rain, I hack
at slippery boards all morning,
jump on them, break them
over my knee, the textbook
tenderfoot—foresight! foresight!—
scrambling now to save myself,
and hearing Nels's voice:

"When the wood's dry, *that's*
when ya cut it 'n stack it.
Not when it's soakin wet!"

"Good weather, plan for rain.
Gotta know what y're about b'y!"

arm-load by arm-load I stack my
soggy splits around the stove,
in the oven, up the wall,
keeping a careful relay:

burning wood. to dry wood.
to burn.

burning wood. to dry wood.
to burn.

◆

Night on the island is full of power. In the dark the land and sea are released from the spell of logic and industry the sun's light places upon them. The water, the trees and hills rise up. They roam and assume what shape they wish.

At one point last night I stepped out of the cabin and was startled by the gigantic glaring presence of the moon, its reflection reaching in a broad flashing path down the sea, like a river of cold light falling straight to the cabin door. I had never seen the moon so large or so white, and its light seemed too sharp, too keen and alert: as if grinning—not hungrily exactly—but with knowing, exultant power, like some great animal.

It moved briskly, this creature of light, rippling its body with easy energy. And I stood swallowed up, gazing into it. But I could not bear it for long. It was too massive and too cold to confront alone. In a rush I turned back to the cabin and opened the door: the relief! the lantern throwing its cone of warm light over the table, my book, the woodstove crackling contentedly.

◆

having no shovel and
no knife long enough
I prowl the slippery wreckage
of one old house
find a leg from a vanished stove

and wade far out on the tide flats
my raincoat hood screening all but the
squishing kelp
the barnacled stones crackling under foot.

alone in drizzle, I stop.
sniff raw salt.
the low sea before me broad as the edge of the world.
behind: black rubble shore. half
hidden in mist.
a few gulls sliding slowly across.

I hum
warm in the pleasure of hunting.
eyes on the bubbling sand.
dig fast. lever the heavy iron

but only bring them up broken
fat clams all gone to rags.
a stupid waste.
I throw the stove leg away and
hunch. dig like an animal
ramming sand under my nails
spade my fingers around the plump shells.
strain.
drag the muscular buggers up
their white flesh still bulging
leaking juice

♦

on the bunk, behind the stove,
every bowl and pan catching
drips, I make my rounds as if
tapping a sugar bush, empty
them all in a pail and open the door
to pitch it—rain gusting in—
I stop. seeing the cabin's afloat
in a giant pool. mountain runoff
pouring under the back wall
gurgling out at the steps. I close
the door hearing my father's voice
his solid Ontario disbelief:
"they built it in the middle of a
bog for cats' sake! And the roof!
Man-oh-man." (in real grief)
"The flashing's on *top* of the shingles!
All the rain goes *inside!*"

I stand listening like a boy
embarrassed
ashamed to have any connection
with such a place

having no excuse that would convince *him*
no practical explanation why
people here set so little store
in staying high and dry.

◆

4th day of hurricane. (3? No, 4 for sure.) Time gone to mush cooped in here nursing a fire. Hum, talk a lot, bake biscuits, wash myself, socks, towels, keep plenty of water hot, staggering out to the spring, buckets whirling my arms like a carnival ride.

Sat most of today at the table. Dusk from the time I got up. The drips, the walls jumping forward. Feel myself getting like the potatoes, soft, sprouty. Even my head changing shape. Wind wearing me down. Don't fight it I tell myself. Go with it. Join it. It'll get tired by and by.

Night again. Hissing lamp. Windows black as obsidian. Rattling sleet. Eat I'm telling my body. Fuel for the night. But it gazes down like an eagle perched in a cage. Jellied chicken and carrots. Cold on a plate. My body looks away.

The radio. Batteries weak. Tipping it up and down, I get the marine weather, listen close, expecting emergency bulletins, ships sunk, men lost at sea. The guy's prim voice patters on about moderate southerly winds. No word of a northeast hurricane. Where the hell is he? Broadcast booth in the heart of a bomb shelter?

I pace around blocked, bottled, can't ask, can't reach out, summons, contact, move. Can't budge. Can't change a thing.

The cabin cartwheels into the night. Black end-of-the-world ocean. Miles and miles. Not a light. Not a man.

♦

ducks swoop low over the
near beach as I breast the tall
weeds, stepping
carefully among the spiky planks
around these broken dwellings

no doors attached, no
glass in the windows, I look in
on fallen ceilings, iron beds, chairs
crushed under avalanches of lath.

where have they gone
the people who carved the air here
with their births and funerals
their scurried visits along the windy paths?

where have their children scattered to?

the grass still rustles with their parents' voices,
people who tried to balance their homes
between water and air.

◆

who were these people?
what did they make of this place?
were they always thinking of somewhere else as
home? Ireland, St. John's, clattering streets, sun?
was this a break, a long side-loop in their lives?
a chance to get rich on fish?
a way to survive until something better beckoned?
were they lost? baffled? blown here they didn't
know how?
were they home here, planted and satisfied, Eden's
humble attempters? the cod and ducks and berries
limits to the only world they hungered for?

so little left to speak for them.
white stones in the boggy burying ground, a few
small houses fallen in. rich plots of weeds.
a path leading nowhere under gulls.

what about it, you young girls, you old women?
what did you dream at night with the fire out
and wind tugging the roof?
ice? an ocean of ice closing the island round?
green glimmering mountains grinding the island down?

was it summer you dreamt of? split fish spread
in the sun? dresses and shoes for Sunday paths?
courting in meadows? bells in the blue air?
your babies, your sweet curly heads, their tiny
fingers clinging?

was it wood stacked in a shed you saw, the stove
fat and red? your family's faces around the supper
lamp, their backs a wall to the night?

whatever you dreamed, you are gone.

your dreams gone too.

◆

I walk around the cabin, the stage
and wharf of Carm Denny, the last
man to live on the island. out here
years after everyone else had gone.
first with his mother, and then she
died and their place burned down
and he stayed on in this hut by the shore
until the police came and took him away.

I lift the latch and step into
the slatted shade of his stage.
cracks and flashing water underneath.
everything still strong and neat.
good hand-cut timbers. wire
and poles and bits of iron-scrap
all sorted and stacked or
hung along the walls.
a lifetime of saving this and that.

the dark-stained cutting table
stands by a wall, its top
hollowed and curved as a woman's back.
a little trap door opens to
empty the offal into the waves.
all nicely arranged for gutting his catches
out of the weather.

and where is he now? shot full
of sedative in some bed or chair.
nothing at all in his head or hands.
his life, his whole work broken off
smashed by our superior tidiness
as though it's a favour to him to have
stopped him from meeting once and for all

whatever was hunting him
or on some blue winter day
letting the ringing hills be
the very last bit of what he knew.

♦

Steady rain all day and the air still. Sweeping the cabin this
morning I lifted a piece of linoleum and found a trap door,
the entrance to Carm's root cellar—just a hole in the rock
really, neatly packed with peat. All that seemed to be down
there at first was mummified potatoes, and then I noticed a
biscuit tin set back on a ledge under the cabin floor. Inside
the tin was a Bible, and in the Bible a photograph of a girl. I
took these up into the light and spent a long time looking at
them, wondering why they were there. The girl, seen from
the waist up, is standing against a white clapboard wall. She
is wearing a kerchief and a dark coat buttoned to the throat.
Her hair, where it shows at her forehead and above one
shoulder, is black. She is handsome, her face lean, her jaw
and cheekbones strong. Her eyes are large and dark by the
look of it. But there is no light in her face, no smile, no
desire to please. She is not angry, nor is she frightened or
withdrawn into herself, but she is guarded all the same. She
does not like whoever is looking at her. I would guess she is
eighteen or nineteen. There is nothing written on the back.

The red ribbon book mark and the photo were both at the
same place in the Bible: Genesis 32, all about Jacob's travels.
I thought about keeping the Bible up to read, but finally
decided to put it back where I found it, the tin tightly shut
and the photo inside.

◆

Carm

I wasn't always alone like people think. The year after my
mother died a boat coming late from the Labrador called in
here. Had lost its fresh water in a gale and needed to make
repairs, so they anchored in the bay and they used my wharf,
and twice they had supper with me. There was a girl among
them, had been all summer making fish on the Labrador, and
I took a liking to her. She was straight and beautiful and I
knew she liked my place by the way she stood at the
window, the way she touched the lamp, the chair, and I said
to her right out you'll stay with me won't you, and I showed
her what I had for the winter, potatoes and turnips under the
floor, fish in the stage, flour and butter and that, and showed
where my dad's house used to be, the black ashes still there,
and I said I was saving to build it up again, a two-storey
house with windows over the bay. And she said she'd stay.
And the night before they sailed, her uncle who was captain
and head of the crew paid her off and married us right here.
We put our hands on the Bible, and it was done.

The fish was still running here then and every day I was
working bringing them in, and my God that woman could
work too, and we scarcely spoke together for over a week.
And then one night she started to talk to me. Her father had
been a mariner out of Trinity Bay. When she was seven years
old he was lost at sea and her mother had no means of
keeping her youngsters fed, so they went to the aunts and
uncles. Some to St. John's, some to Placentia Bay. Her
mother died of consumption when she was ten. She
remembered it all so clearly still. The way her mother had
cried saying goodbye to her. And she said she hated the uncle
that took her in.

That winter didn't last any time at all. She used to go with
me everywhere, back over the island for ptarmigan and for
timber to ship around in the spring. And at night we'd talk
and sing together—and the songs that woman knew! The
hundreds of songs she knew! In the spring though she didn't
want people to know she was here. If anyone came ashore
she'd go and hide. Once we heard voices right close to the
house and she quick got into the turnip cellar under the
floor. I tried to tell her it didn't matter a sheep's fart, but she
wouldn't have people looking at her, people I knew from
Conche and Englee is what she meant. I don't know what the
reason for that was. By ourselves we were happy as birds.

When the baby was on its way I was some glad. Made a
small bed from young spruce and painted it green. A son or
daughter, it didn't matter which. The problem was she
couldn't be having the baby alone. I said I'd get a woman
from Englee when the time was near. But she wouldn't agree.
Wanted to go to some people of hers in St. John's. And when
a boat bound that way came by they took her along. She told
me she'd write, and I was going to go when the season was
done and bring her home. And a letter came then after a
couple months, a letter her aunt had wrote saying my wife
was dead. My wife and our baby both. I went with the man
who'd carried the letter out, and got to St. Anthony, and
finally a boat from there to St. John's. And I found the house
of the aunt. But the woman looked at me like I was lord of
the plague. Made me stand in the door and all she would say
was my wife and child were buried down to the Belvedere. I
went and walked through the rows of crosses and stones, the
snow on the ground then. Her name wasn't anywhere. At
the big cathedral I spoke with the man with the books and
lists of names and he told me he had no record of her being
buried there. The bitch of an aunt didn't want to see me
again but I pounded and pounded and made her open the
door, and she handed me out a photograph of my wife and

said to go back to the graveyard again, the girl was gone for sure the same as the uncle was. And she shut the door in my face and that was that.

I took the train across the island then, my only time on a train, all the ponds and barrens covered in snow, and I traveled by snow machine and dog team down from Deer Lake to Englee. But nobody wanted to go to the Grey Islands by then with the coves freezing across. I spent the rest of the winter with people in Englee, cutting wood in the bush and mending nets. I never told anyone why I'd been gone. I was waiting, that's all, waiting and seeing my house that I couldn't get back to. Empty. Frozen and dark.

◆

Was on the water most of the day with the Wellons. Cyril asked three days ago if I'd ever seen a cod trap being pulled, said they'd be by to get me next trip out. I heard their boat at seven this morning and jumped out of bed, no time to eat, went out the door pulling my sweater on and that was the start. Even now, ten at night, the cabin is flowing and tipping, the floor like a breathing belly. I close my eyes and: codfish, body to body, eyes, mouths gaping. Walls of stirring life.

◆

these *birds* again. skimming
the water gullies all their lives

dodging the grabbing waves until
they can't.

and that's okay.

slipping into the only thing
they ever looked at

the thing they were only ever
an inch above.

◆

up. down. up. down.
cliffs and the burly cove do
giant sit-ups, boards underfoot
shy, dodge, my boots shooting away
in the blood and water (with Cyril
steadily lifting, hauling the line)
I sprawl scramble for someplace to
brace my feet hitting the
engine house I reach out catch
the turning capstan bar—Pete
pushing the other end—I hang on
help twist the capstan creaking around
drawing the trapline tight the long
skiff tipping pressed down with
the weight and nothing giving
nothing coming up the birch capstan
breaks off in our hands the line dives
back into the sea.

"She's some fierce tide," Cyril says.
He throws the broken capstan into the bow.
"We'll try again in an hour's time."

◆

knees on the rolling gunnels
we lean out drawing the trap up slowly
hand over hand, lifting a thousand
fish in a tightening house.

something boiling begins to emerge,
one, two tails turn
swelling the surface, then
long backs braiding smoothly rise
clear to the light as we claw more and more
of their mesh walls away from them.

Cyril is dancing, already guessing
how many thousand pounds as he jabs
the dip net among them yanking
thudding their slippery bodies into the skiff
he digs wildly ripping the air through his
teeth, making a rainbow of fish
white bellies, eyes, mouths
wide with amazement going by in a blur, he
works like a man in a fairy tale
who is shown a mountain of gold
and told he can keep whatever he digs in a day.

◆

five tons of fish slippery as
pumpkin seeds on the longliner's deck,
I lift my foot high and wade
into them, feeling their bodies press
my sinking legs, stepping
on eyes and bellies, things
I usually treat so carefully.

two splitting tables ready to go,
Cyril gives me a knife and shows
how to slit the throats just
back of the gills then run the
blade down the belly seam to the tail.

I do this, passing the opened fish
to Ross who tries to twist their
heads off on the table's edge
the way Cyril tells him to. but
some of these fish having
necks thick as a wrist, Ross
struggles and Cyril shows him again
using his weight, using the table's
edge, until he gets it down pat.

taking the fish last, Cyril
moves his knife twice, down
one side of the spine and back with
a quick jerk, stripping the spine away
like a chain of ice,
his blade never touching the meat,
laid flat now, the white
triangular ware, the Newfoundland trade,

and he skids that into a barrel
for Pete to scrub.

the table's old wood gets
plush with blood then ridged
in grey scum and Pete sloshes
a bucket of water under our hands
and the scuppers gradually clog and we
move knee-deep in fish and blood
a thick pool washing heads and entrails
under us and blood drips from our jackets
spatters our faces and dries and
spatters our faces again, and I squeeze
my gloved hands and the fat and blood
pour out of them like gravy
and all around the air is flashing
white gulls, shrill with their crazy
hunger, wheeling, diving to
fight for the floating guts.

all this life being
hacked apart, us letting
blood out of its envelopes,
the world suddenly seems to be all
alive, blood running inside
of us and outside of us, inside
our hands and over them, with little
between the two, a cover of skin
keeping me in or out I'm not
sure which, but some sharp
bones have gone into my hands
and some of the running blood is mine.

◆

I use Carm's brook only for fresh water now, having learned to fish straight from the sea. I find the sea-run trout always thick off the point for some reason and eager to take the lure. The water I get for drinking is clear brown, nearly as dark as tea, and it tastes of the island, the rocks and peat, years underground.

◆

A strange shaking comes over me here at the end, knowing
the end is near. Frost on the grass this morning, the sky's
sharp blue soaked into everything, and I know going south
I'll be going back in time, back into warmer days and I need
that now, trembling at how I'll change being with Karen
again, back into flesh and blood, time thickening, slowing
me down, letting me out of the spear point narrowing line
this place is paring me to.

◆

a small crack first in the morning's
spell. the tall clarity, wind and sea
and birds' talk thinly mixing, holding
everything in a blue shell, and then?
a speck. a gust. crows' clatter far
at the edge? some faint hammering
some coarse-toothed saw making a hole,
a sound I recognize, and I'm out of
the cabin the end of land at my feet
and low in the blue curve beyond the
last shimmering line, eastern light
is catching a boat's white face and
I'm shaking now knowing the slow
gravelly beat with Nels at its centre
staring into the sun, and I'm
inside throwing things into a bag,
home, Karen, my children, their
faces their bodies and running once
more to the brook the blunt speech
of peat my feet do not move, my arms
have gone over my head, waving as Nels
ploughs closer down the blue hill

That Night We Were Ravenous

THE SEA GANGS IN –

darkly faceted,
eager,
yakking and glancing around at the jewellery-shop shelves,
then, lifting arms that darken the air,
sweeps everything to its chest.

It opens its mouth
and clearly wants food.

The sea gangs in gay and pointy,
weed green;
the smell of it gives you hungry lungs;
its thud feels good as fucking;

then it drags the stones of the beach back, rattling them,
all the bones people have left, skulls
empty of pleasures,
ownerless teeth.

The sea gangs in
buttered with morning light, throwing its lace hem at your
    bachelor's boots,
and you snap photos, kneeling,
panting,
pen poems,

and the waves, as they draw themselves up to dive,
for a second,
go thin and glassy,
give glimpses into a place where pale shapes tilt and stretch
like long green boxes
in a stone cell.

CEDAR COVE

If your wharf is washed away
it will come to Cedar Cove—
Wild Cove on the maps or
Capelin Cove. If your boat

goes down it will sail to Cedar
Cove piece by piece.
And your uncle, should he not come back
from his walk on Cape St. George,

will be found grinning among
the glitter of barkless roots
laths struts stays
stringers and frayed rope

in Cedar Cove, where no
cedars have ever grown,
but that's what the local people
call it. The water horizon

topples straight down
on Cedar Cove over
and over, box cars
falling, loads of TNT.

And the wind will not let you speak
in Cedar Cove, which could
be called Deaf Cove
or Lobotomy Cove, will not

let you think or stand straight;
the shrunk trees writhe
and have the wrong kinds
of leaves, but their roots spread

wide in Cedar Cove,
whose gravel is soft compared
to its air. We have come to Cedar
Cove overland, my love

and I, having been lost
at sea in another way.
All day we scatter
ourselves through the noise

and whiteness, learning the thousand
ways things can be taken
apart and reassigned—
the boot sole impaled on the shattered

trunk, the rust flakes,
the bone flakes encrusting a bracelet
of kelp—losing our pictures
of home, stick by stick.

After Cedar Cove,
how will we look?

LONG POINT

cosmographer's dream of perspective

past Lourdes, past
Black Duck Brook the peninsula's
limestone spine tapers for fifteen miles northeast
into the Gulf of St. Lawrence

road into whitecaps and air

shedding its margins

road to the loss of road   out
of solidity

I walk that windy spit to its vanishing point
where opposing surfs merge
where Port au Port Bay and its sky and its weather
lose to the open gulf
and the slick whittled rock I stand on plunges
titanic eel

for a long time I lean letting my face ride like a kite
on the turbulence

wave noise twists
to a throat I could slip through in a dive

part of me does dive,
I feel tracings, shadows go with the strong pull
out of my skin

into another place
where I must be walking even now

TRAVELLER'S GUIDE TO THE GEOLOGY OF NEWFOUNDLAND AND LABRADOR

with thanks to Stephen Colman-Sadd and Susan Scott

Drive to Moreton's Harbour, and take the road
that circles the east side of the harbour
warm air through the open windows, I drive
with a hand half under your loose shorts, your

leg a warm vein of gold *turn left onto a*
gravel road that continues around the harbour,
and park where a picket fence encloses two
satellite dishes hair loose on your cheek,

your eyes fix on the unfurling bay, then you
read again *walk along the path between*
the fence and the high rocky hill; it crosses
the neck to some old fenced fields from the back

of the seat my fingers fall into your hair,
discover your spine's soft nuggets *as you enter*
Little Harbour, note the rough flow texture
of the lava on your right (my heart's needle

leaping) *and the smooth glacially polished*
and fluted diabase outcrops on your left
we carry our lunch over the old convulsions,
crackling lichen, crabs' claws dropped

by gulls *beyond the fields on the shore,*
and best seen at low tide, are pillows,
and splattered volcanic ash and lava fragments
wind flutters the pages, flutters your blue

top, my hand sails lightly in that sea
the beds have been folded so they are nearly
vertical and compression has formed a cleavage
almost at right angles to the bedding I kneel

smelling the basalt, the rhyolite hot
in the sun, the pegmatite dikes, smell
of old burning *small holes in some of the*
rocks were once gas bubbles in the molten

lava I spread the blanket, carefully
place the oranges, the plums on the jagged
stones *these features indicate an explosive*
volcanic environment you close the book.

We both look at the sea

FOR MY EXECUTION

For my execution,
the spot I choose is just to the south
of where the barn used to stand, a zone
where the grass rippled and posed like a handsome animal,
sleek on a century of barnyard loam,

where our horse, Pat, lay down one Saturday morning
and I sat on his flank grinning and squinting into the
east to have my picture taken
and he didn't care,

my sister, housecoated, holding the camera, her neck
and shoulders bitten away by the sun, the milk-house
beside her with its unused well under
a clutter of planks,
the fieldstone throat I would peer down, into
the past, watching a pebble fall—once in a drought,
to water the garden, my father pumped out its
stench, its corpses, liquid blots of fur—

a spot I wanted only to leave,
the cedar rail paddock we built in a bad
mood, the tramped grass steamy as seaweed in the migraine
of noon, lending myself like a slave as we
dug the holes,
postponing my ownership,
reserving my willingness
for my own life, somewhere over the rim of that ploughed
green bowl.

I will kneel and wait for it,
facing east.

ECLIPSE AGAIN

So hard to parcel an event
without lying. A flood running *out*
in every direction, including up and down, an
ignition, a flowering, a turning inside out, an animal
busy in the wild, and you decide tick
tack toe connect the dots across this thing,
and that represents it all?
We can extrapolate the rest?
It's true,
old boxes, old jars
hum with a kind of diffused meaning, old
medieval coffers, Tang bowls hold so much more
than wine or thimbles or emptiness. Words
too are like that,
the old standard containers you crack your mind
into like an egg. Even choosing
a chain of events is an equally old language,
even saying "I" and "it"
and "happened," the old customs are there.
But it wasn't *like* that,
there was no climax and denouement,
or there *was*, but the denouement was a climax too
and the story went on in another direction, which
my ghost, watching from under the water inside my heart,
found more interesting, more
significant.
With the eclipse coming on and me running to find
Shawn to be together at the astronomical tourist attraction,
the cosmic wedding photograph,
it suddenly hit me
that I was leaving my daughter at home,
that she had told me that morning she'd dreamt
of the eclipse—that she'd burnt her eyes looking at it—
and we had talked about how, when she was very young,

she had worried that our cat would be blinded in the back
yard during an eclipse in Pasadena, Newfoundland,
and it hit me that maybe she wanted me to be with her again
poking a hole in a playing card to catch the black sun
on an envelope,
and I was abandoning her,
so when I found Shawn, we turned
and walked quickly home, me carrying the milk, past
a mother duck minding fifteen newly hatched ducklings,
past woods full of trilliums, under the coral
buds on the maples, among the spooky
blurred shadows, home,
where we acted as if nothing strange was going on,
where we washed dishes and I made a pinhole in cardboard
that didn't work
and we talked about what movies were coming,
about playing pool, about getting
into university.

PRIMITIVE RENAISSANCE

We travel south to a shore crackling
and aromatic, necklaced in salt,

then to an island,
white,
giddy in space, where shoes
shirts, jeans wander off on their own and skin

remembers its language, bounds
into conversation with the world, skilled in a grammar it
never learned in the north,

sniffing,
yanking us off the path. Every object it meets
is its physical kin,

has a shapely ass
or anecdotes, invitations to meals.

At the sun-scarred table, heat
rustles the eucalyptus leaves overhead, pine
and oregano spirits brushing us.

My fingers find the cup's tiny
shape deep in its own white glare. Inspired,

we plan a high culture built
low to the ground,
a primitive renaissance.

Looking at you, I have never felt so wholly
at home in a country of pupils
and lips.

It comes around, if you let it.
The land comes around
inside the eyes.

Under the table, our starved feet are
pigging the cinnamon dust.

THE GREEN INSECT

I had a green insect, a kind that had never before been seen,
descendant of an ancient nation, regal, rigid in ritual.

It would sun itself on my windowsill, stretching its legs one by one,
        its hinged joints, its swivel joints, its claws,
unfolding and folding its Swiss army knife implements.
It was ready for a landing on the moon.

Around my page it marched itself like a colour guard.
It halted, and its segments fell into place, jolting all down the line.

It uncased its wings, which glistened the way sometimes very old
        things glisten: tortoiseshell fans, black veils, lantern glass.

It was a plant with a will, an independent plant, an early invention
        wiser than what we've arrived at now.
It was a brain coiled in amulets for whom nature is all hieroglyphs.

People gawked, and a woman pointed a camera, and I hesitated,
        but—I did—I held the insect up by its long back legs like a
        badge, like my accomplishment,
and the air flashed, and the insect twisted and fought, breaking its
        legs in my fingertips, and hung

lunging, fettered with stems of grass,
and I laid it gently down on a clean page,
but it wanted no convalescence,
it ripped up reality, it flung away time and space,
I couldn't believe the strength it had,

it unwound its history, ran out its spring in kicks and rage, denied
        itself, denied me and my ownership, fizzed, shrank, took off in
        wave after wave of murder,
        and left nothing but this page faintly stained with green.

TELL ME I'M NOT MAKING THIS UP

The time we were married, it was spring,
we were just into our twenties and a fierce
excitement was in the air, like the world was going to
reveal itself in some glorious way that summer
and only a fool or bloodless slave would have chosen
to stick with a city job—fluorescent shifts
in a sealed-window office block sort of thing—
and we got what they called a "drive-away" car
to take west, that was before the Japanese
import boom, and second-hand cars were worth more
in Alberta than in the east, so we picked up a V-8
Buick to drop off in Edmonton, just for the cost
of the gas, which was dirt cheap then too,
and we headed out for the prairies, which neither
of us had seen and the Rockies and the west
coast of Vancouver Island which is still a dream,
the Pacific rolling with life, the whole Orient
curling against the body of North America,
the luminous air, the distances you could see
that summer, but what sticks in my mind most
troublingly, like a glimpse of magic, the
epitome of the time, was that crossing the plains,
in our living-room suite on wheels, we kept
passing guys on motorbikes also headed
west on the straight flat stretches of empty road
who were just sitting there, perched
or reclining on their machines like fakirs
on flying carpets, not holding the handlebars,
not touching any controls. One guy was riding
side-saddle, his legs crossed, reading a book.
He grinned and waved as we rocketed past,
upholstery up to our ears.
Another was lying back on his bed-roll, hands

folded behind his neck, ankles on top of the
headlight, his shadow skimming below—fifty
miles an hour under the continent's sky,
ignoring the facts of physics.

The summer was rich in displays like that.

Where are you anti-gravity riders now?
You mockers of laws? Write to me care of
Grenfell College, Corner Brook. Tell me I'm
not making this up.

GRANARY

In those rainy villages the people
kept their grain dry in wooden
granaries on stilts, steep-roofed
cabins like sacred storks,
but rats could scoot straight up
the stilts and steal, and cloud
the whole year's meals with their
insulting stink; so the people
attached skirts of wood high
on each stilt—the barrel-makers
made these skirts of fine-grained
ash, waxed so no rats' claws
could get a grip on them—and
on a patch of flagstones under
each granary, they put a house
for a dog, with an intelligent
terrier in front and a little
sign over the arched door bearing
his name—*Antony* or *Fidelio*—
and title: *Guardian of the Grain*,
so he'd be proud and diligent
in his war on the rats. To enter
the granaries, mostly the people used
oak ladders which they religiously
took down from the granary doors
and hung crossways on pegs fixed
in the stilts; sometimes they
worked out hinged sets of stairs
counterbalanced with a rock at the
top—with an easy tug on a strap,
even a child could tip these stairs
down and bring back a basket of grain.

THAT NIGHT WE WERE RAVENOUS

Driving from Stephenville in the late October
dusk—the road swooping and disappearing ahead
like an owl, the hills no longer playing dead
the way they do in the daytime, but sticking their black
blurry arses up in the drizzle and shaking themselves,
heaving themselves up for another night of
leapfrog and Sumo ballet—some

trees detached themselves from the shaggy
shoulder and stepped in front of the car. I swerved

through a grove of legs startled by pavement, maybe a
hunchbacked horse with goiter, maybe a team of beavers
trying to operate stilts: it was the

landscape doing a moose, a cow
moose,
most improbable forest device. She danced
over the roof of our car in moccasins.

She had burst from the zoo of our dreams and was
there, like a yanked-out tooth the dentist
puts in your hand.

She flickered on and off.
She was strong as the Bible and as full of lives.
Her eyes were like Halley's Comet, like factory whistles,
like bargain hunters, like shy kids.

No man had touched her or given her movements geometry.

She surfaced in front of us like a coelacanth, like a face
in a dark lagoon. She made us feel blessed.

She made us talk like a cage of canaries.

She reminded us. She was the ocean wearing a fur suit.

She had never eaten from a dish.
She knew nothing of corners or doorways.

She was our deaths come briefly forward to say hello.

She was completely undressed.

She was more part of the forest than any tree.
She was made of trees. The beauty of her face was bred
in the kingdom of rocks.

I had seen her long ago in the Dunlap Observatory.

She leapt from peak to peak like events in a ballad.

She was insubstantial as smoke.

She was a mother wearing a brown sweater opening her arms.

She was a drunk logger on Yonge Street.

She was the Prime Minister. She had granted us a tiny reserve.

She could remember a glacier where she was standing.

She was a plot of earth shaped like the island of
Newfoundland and able to fly, spring down in the middle of
cities scattering traffic, ride elevators, press pop-eyed
executives to the wall.

She was charged with the power of Churchill Falls.

She was a high-explosive bomb loaded with bones and meat. She broke the sod in our heads like a plough parting the earth's black lips.

She pulled our zippers down.
She was a spirit.

She was Newfoundland held in a dam. If we had touched her, she would've burst through our windshield in a wall of blood.

That night we were ravenous. We talked, gulping, waving our forks. We entered one another like animals entering woods.

That night we slept deeper than ever.

Our dreams bounded after her like excited hounds.

New Poems

SOUR FIRE

Those determined middle-aged
men whose marriages have failed
and who've taken to the outdoors
and puff alone along trails
with their backpacks and their practical shapeless hats—
I do not want to be one of them.

I do not want to have everything I need
in a van,
drawers that open under the bed,
shelves that flop down.
I do not want to park on a wharf
eating my tin of stew.

Because he always yearned to go camping, but
the wife wasn't so keen (although she made an effort
and there are photos of her in a plaid shirt
drinking whisky from a mug near a lot of smoke),
and now she's left,
and I don't want this museum-house, each
item in it swollen with past,
tender, cut by the slightest glance, the memories
spurting—
her painted birds over the bed: they plucked
Ruth out of the air, but wherever they're flying
I'm still going down
down—
the masculine hinterland beckons.

But I don't want to join the trekkers trying
to repudiate houses and towns
and the work that creates them
as though they're all dedicated to women.

This man squatting alone by a sour fire,
bitten by flies,
telling himself he's getting close to the truth,
is not me.

HELIX

When we take off for Amsterdam in the rain and high
mist we're instantly over the University of Montreal
and the green mountain, which is flat, and I'm looking
straight down on the Jacques Cartier bridge, the docks
where thirty-five years ago I got on the *Yildun*
and sailed as a deck-hand to Holland—confused
to be suddenly at the railing of time's helix, seeing
my younger self from this unforeseeable ledge.
There's the current that swept us downstream when
we cast off and the engines failed, our dead-duck
German freighter finally crashing sideways into
an American ship. I braced and watched the two
hulls buckle, then groaning spring back into shape.
Our flight goes north-east back over the route
I drove last week from Newfoundland, over the Gulf
which I crossed on the *Yildun* in '66. The plane's
videos show a map of Newfoundland with a dot
marked Corner Brook and a red arrow, which is us,
inching into it, and I feel this arrow carry me
through my own heart—for twenty-six years my home
has been down there—carry me through the heart
of my ex-wife who is there now—my vows and the leap
of my dreams' trajectory somehow cut off and me
flying up here, going to meet my new love in Vienna,
going to Poland, while half my soul is down there,
baffled, glimpsing its own gnomic face in the windows
of passing cars. How does the mind get taken apart
like this, a trio, a quartet tentatively playing,
tuning, playing, looser and looser and more true
as it breaks up over the sea among the clouds
that are half dark, half catching the sliding light?

When Cook came ashore here, his heart rose
and advanced like the boat that brought him,
riding on water so clear he might have been
sailing in sky, and the white sand he squinted at
and the green curls hanging plaited with red
hibiscus confirmed in his mind that God shared
his ideal of feminine beauty, since it burgeoned
forth in women and antelopes, fern-trees, even
in whole islands like this formed far from
jaded Europe in boundless blue. Having seen
the like in Tahiti and the many coral or smoking
islands on his way, he was already sure this
wasn't the southern continent. It rode too
lightly on the sea to carry massive commerce,
rivers of iron and brick, but then you never knew,
there might be gold, or wood to fashion ships
that wouldn't rot. And the excitement of Banks
and Solander, now crowding the dinghy's prow,
was always contagious; they had already spotted
birds they didn't recognise; would be in the water
before the boat touched land. No matter that
the natives, when they met them, would undoubtedly
be thieves, as proud of murder as of any art
they had, and that there would be venomous things
in the thickets; the world held marvels like
the legends said. By now he was mapping dreams.

BIRD SONGS IN THE TWO BAYS OF ISLANDS

The New Zealand Bay of Islands birds whistle long
and elastic, then twist and bulge into rich chuckles
and clicks—portly ventriloquists on a greased trapeze.

Birds in the Newfoundland Bay of Islands sound wistful
and distant no matter how close they are, *lonely me me me
me,*
or they bark from high up, echoing rock and ice,
recommending matter, cold
marrow, tipping the head back—breath a brief shadow,
unrelated to light.

The air over the gardens that fall away
from our window to Navarino Bay is festooned
with the talk of unseen birds. The cypresses
and the Malta plums, whose clusters of green fruit
puzzled us—not figs, not apricots—harbour
them in their shadows, birds who want to be known
only in sound, strutting in tight trills,
cinch-belt whistles, yellow rickrack for the ear.
This morning, walking the cliff-side road into town,
I found a tiny plain bird with a broken wing
trying to hurry along in the roadside mallow.
And coming back with raisin bread and cherry jam
and two pieces of loukoumia to go with our coffee,
I met a carefully dressed old man moving his polished
shoes without any help, the nearly spent
fire of some disease deep in his face,
his remarkable moustache and eyebrows like three small
huskies pulling him out of his bed into
the street, while a woman, maybe his daughter, at a little
distance waited for him, distressed, disapproving,
annoyed with his determination to walk
on his own, when he couldn't walk, when he barely offered
enough of a structure to support his clothes.

WATERFRONT

On the roof of the Kruger mill, a tiny
man is working among piles of . . . I raise
the binoculars . . . planks. He cuts planks
on a bench with a saw fixed to it, puts
the pieces on a hand-cart, adds a roll
of roofing felt, and wheels his materials
over the tar desert. Shadows cast by
the smoke tumble across him, then he's
again in sun, chopped up in glare.
Downwind, even at this range the mill's
flues and blowholes roar like a kicked ear.
Smoke boils from the stack at the speed
of the background waves riding up Humber Arm—
flecks of sun, flecks of foam on their crests—
the speed of the back and forth forklift
loading newsprint on a ship. Houses glint
in the south shore hills. Beyond, the Blomidons
rise, sky-blended, brown. Behind sky.

my left nostril over the sea coast, the winter
mountains and forests of west Newfoundland—
Port au Port to Cow Head—
I snuff up the dry dust of black spruce boughs
sweetened with fine snow,

and salt water's cold chowder aroma.

Extra sinuses open.

inhale lone cars on the narrow plowed roads,
their tickle acrid like certain bugs,

millsmoke,

the smell of a thousand people going somewhere in a trance,

breathe up myself walking, shouting, stopping to jot in a book,
shouting,
jotting,
making an echo map of the Blomidons,

from small muffled barks behind Benoit's Cove ("hey!"
no repetitions)

westward along the peridotite slopes

until sharp three-syllable declarations
("going home!")
bounce back to me three times below Pissing Horse Falls

SMOKE

To still be driving the familiar roads
when your family has gone—every object
gives off past like evening rocks
shedding their daytime heat. Mount Moriah,
Rattling Brook, Bottle Cove: encyclopaedias
opening at a glance. You ghost, you deep
sea diver. Every twig behind glass.
We all talked at once passing along
here, someone reaching into the back seat
for the thermos, someone clattering
in a bag of cassettes, streak of colours
left hanging over the pavement, old aviary
on wheels, travelling bonfire, smoke
you sniffing lost dog now pass through

SEVEN

Does it help to think of the number seven?

There was the cow with a perfect white seven
on her black forehead who would cross German Mills
Road and graze outside the school, and we would
spill out at recess, crying, "Number Seven's here!"

Alone in bed now with the light on, trying
different turnings.

Are there seven stages to sleep,
seven rungs,
seven chances and I used mine up?

Come into my bedroom, Number Seven, still chewing,
swishing your tail.
Since neither your farm nor your owner, Bill Denby,
can be found in their old locations, I open my home
to you,
        amazed
that you followed me all the way from school
to stand at the foot of my bed,
big-boned,
shyly tenaciously watching me as you used to do
with your human inhuman eyes.

BLOMIDON TWIN

I had no way of knowing it then
but the man sleeping below me
in the bunk in the youth hostel
in Brussels in 1966, whose face
I never saw, was an early version
of the Blomidon Mountains—the
geological Siamese twin which,
ten years later, I would discover
I had. He snored, he made the ten
thousand sounds of the ocean
with his mouth, he made ranges
of mountains, and I lay fitting
images to that Caliban's racket,
sleepless in Hieronymus Bosch's
hell. Now I've met my twin in these
bald mountains. I try to walk
normally in their contradictory winds,
wondering why I can't move away,
loving their baldness, their liverish
contour lines, their white shapes'
blur on the map on my wall. They
snore and pull a blanket of cloud
down over their eyes, they stink of
dry mouth, they are ugly when they
think of certain things and forget
that others are watching them.

What used to worry me most about death
was the prospect of being separated
from you, sealed up alone in a black
box forever, or lost in a crowd
of strangers with empty eye-holes
and scorched hair, endlessly shoving
their cold bodies aside, searching
for the homeland of your face.
But that nightmare has come to pass
on this side of the black river,
and perhaps I should be grateful
that I now share the knowledge of those
rare travellers who descended into
Avernus and returned to the ordinary world
with wonders to tell, however despised
or pitied they were. I know what Orpheus
feels, still standing alone on a corner
with hot eyes, talking, talking,
while the crowds pass. Your radiant
figure dissolved like smoke through my own
fault. I thought of that in the fall
as I waded the aching Fox Island River
at the start of the climb up Lewis Hill,
that cold wide height with caribou
carved on a bone-white cloud
outside of time, and I saw you there
in the rock canyon, in the waterfalls' spray,
in the lit curtains of rain over the sea past
Long Point, ivory-yellow, half
smudged in sun, saw you distant
and disappearing over the Lewis Hills,
leaning away on the earth's curve,
and the Blue Hills and the Blomidons.

First you've got to dig chunks
of iron out of some mountain,
and coal, and the machines you
need to do that have to be huge
and are made of iron and coal, so
how do you start? And you blast
the iron in coke-fired furnaces
and make the steel and pour it
in long solid bars that are then
turned on unimaginable lathes
somewhere else—all the travelling
from here to there in rail cars,
ore, coke and steel and engineered
parts, the rail cars themselves
made of steel —and the twenty-
ton rollers and armatures, dreamt
up by young men with brains made
only of numbers and diagrams, get
sent to the Corner Brook mill
and are set up in rows in a room
big enough to hold Governor's
Island. High windows like valves
for letting in light let in a
different kind of light, echoey,
smelling of electrical sparks,
not Humber Arm light, and this
light of Pittsburgh or Stelco
gleams on the perfect steel gods
of the paper machines, the exact
to one ten-thousandth-of-an-inch
twenty-ton milled steel rollers
sleeping in absolute motion.
What do such things do to the space

they lie in? You must worship them
and hate everything you have ever
loved. You must hate your woman,
her body, her words, her smells,
and your desire for her. Hate
what your own childish hand can
fashion. You must hate this god
you now worship, made somewhere
else, in the mysteries of the high
high factories you will never see.

We stop where a steep field mostly
cleared of the wiry spruce rises
up from the water and crosses

the road. Hundreds of boulders,
some sheep. The owner has barred
the way with a gate and run

a stick fence straight up the hill's
side, balanced it there like a twig
on the back of a moose who will

twitch its hide in a minute or take
a step, and you can pick up your twig
and try again or try something

else, stubble, rubble, litter,
grit—the bay's flat white
water, right now at least,

would be a good place to escape
to, waiting for fish in a boat,
looking back at the steep-roofed homes,

the pale road to Curling cutting
the hill's face. The clearings would be
smooth and green from a boat.

"A diesel truck leaves the North Star Cement
Plant at Corner Brook for a load of limestone.
The quarries are a short distance from the plant."

The 1955 sky is modern, the same
unhaunted grey I've known, driving the Ring
Road, walking across the Corner Brook Plaza
parking lot, since 1975.
The card's foreground is a spread of crushed stones
reaching back to the North Star plant, whose long
walls—a middle texture of grey between gravel
and cloud—occupy all the horizon. Wind
pulls the stack's thick smoke straight
east. On the gravel field, leaping before
a torn billow of dust, the diesel truck
is all eagerness, clean, unclotted, young,
its massive tires dismissing the old irritants,
old family troubles the driver might
have had in his head if he were home at the breakfast
table. This strong angel of metallurgy
and math—which by now has rusted to nothing but orange
stains or been melted and cast back into new
boyhood, new engine noise—bounds out
for more of the limestone mountain above Corner
Brook. We will tear everything down and be something
new. Gears and dust-swirls, lunch box, a radio
station—the rest is blank black and white.
The forest, the slow breathing afternoon light
on Humber Arm are crumpled into a tin
foil ball beside the road.

COOK'S LINE

I cut into Cook's pen's
line at latitude 48° 57', longitude 57° 58',
just below his much vandalized
monument
on the edge of Corner Brook.

I lift the section of line extending west
along Humber Arm's south shore.
At first it is no thicker than a thread,
but I flatten it between my palms, I shake it
like a long ribbon, sending
waves down its length.

I tug it from side to side, get it limber
and loose.

The pigment he used was remarkably
dense;
it somehow muffled everything on both sides,
like the Great Wall of China,
kept the smell of the sea out of the land and smell
of the land out of the sea.

I dip the severed line in the salt water
and make it soft,
knead it, stretch it wide like black
dough.

I hold the bottom edge down with my feet spread
wide apart. I stretch
the top corners out with my hands,
making a tunnel, a kind of nighttime road
of Cook's line.

The pigment thins and separates,
you can walk along inside Cook's line
like a long grey cloud.

Listen.

There are French voices inside the line
and voices that might be Micmac
or even Beothuk, men singing in something
like Spanish or Portugese, you can hear
birds and waves among beach stones,
taste the kelpy sound of the surf, clear
serum of mussel juice, clams' fine
squirts.

I take my cassette recording of Alfred saying:
"There's nar fish be d' wharf clar of a sculpin."
and throw that down inside Cook's line.

I take the photos I took of all the groc and confs
and take-outs between Corner Brook
and Lark Harbour and throw them down inside
Cook's line,
              then I throw in the C & E Takeout
itself and the John's Beach church that used to be
in my grade three geography book,
                            and I pick up all
the kids hitchhiking in Mount Moriah
and drive them to the side of Cook's line
and let them out and watch them go
running out of sight in the ink mist,

and I pick up a ball that comes bouncing toward me
in the street in Curling and pitch it
down inside the line, and the ball-hockey players
go chasing after it,
              and the car

that's rocking up and down on its springs
in the bushes just off the Cook's Brook Park
parking lot, I push it slowly into Cook's line
and give it a shove—two startled flushed faces
in the rear window—
                    and I throw in
Woods Island and Pissing Horse Falls
and the solar orgasm rock and Mad Dog Lake
and Lisa and me at the top of Blomidon Head
(Is that a caribou in the pond below? Yes,
it's moving. No, it isn't. Yes, it is.)
and Walt LeMessurier napping in the sun
on the rim of Simms Gorge,
                           and I drag
the line over to the start of the Clark's Brook
road, and a row of skidoos, the riders all
in zipped suits and helmets, roars
down inside Cook's line,
                         and the line
is stretched to bursting now, the inside
spilling back out to the outside, birds'
calls, crinkled light on the bay,
Lorraine with her radio and barbecue—people
in trouble will find her and her help—
Randy and me coming down the scree slope
on the face of the Blomidons, long moonwalk
strides,
         and I know Cook is away down there
somewhere, bent to his table with pen and dividers,
still leaving his fine black trail.

What will he think when his line
spreads and explodes at his pen's
tip and the first of the ball-hockey kids
and skidoos come tumbling in front of him?

Bored with earth's endless business convention in north-east
    Quebec—the black-suited granites huddled, mulling
    their policies,
Humber Arm in a sleeveless dress crosses the cloud-choked Gulf,
    opens an eastern window and reaches out for the feel of
    freshness on her skin,
rain or snow or sunlight, whatever's outside.

Her fine forearm hairs rise in the coolness.

Warm wafts of scent.

Pale in the darkness, she reaches toward you like a path through
    dunes near the sound of surf,
like when the person you're talking to on the phone about the day's
    finished chores, pauses and in a new voice, loosened, open,
    asks, "What are you wearing now?"

Lark Harbour, Gillams, John's Beach, thin bracelets glinting.

The crook of her arm bending slightly backward making a blue-
    veined mound.

Goes on opening windows, entering. Every morning is in your
    bed. Always another bone in your body she wants to learn.

What rustles under her skin is another nature.
Watching her eat a soft-boiled egg you forget that even her
    fingernails are ocean's daughters.

Leaving the street map of her palm, I kiss her wrist's twin tendons,
    like a boat's fresh wake,
climb to the meadow of her upper arm, the musky hollow near
    where her breast begins.

I have slept there in a shrubby dip in the hill above Little Port, my
    face in the gleaming stems of old grass.

I map her imagined shape past her shoulder, past my own reach,
    projecting the probable roots of her smells and rustling,
up the muscles' continued lines, the pivoted sweep of her movements
    to the source of her reaching out,
to her neck and ears, her temples, her hair and eyes,
which I cannot see but can know and remember and cannot stop
    trying to tell about.

Is that a cigarette between her fingers?

I have embraced each of those fingers like tall naked sisters with
    substantial thighs.

A-la-man-a left and *Doe-see-doe*, how many years have we been
    doing this?

Has me eating out of her palm. Snow, which tastes partly chalky,
    partly like apples.
And something remote, ignored, grey, that I know by its taste
        underlies most evolved life, something uninhabited. Long
    before parrots and hibiscus.
I eat this knowledge and grow gaunt, face turned away north like a
    shaggy laird in his cold stone turret.

How many goddesses there must be, like you, slowly swaying your
    five terrible arms in the starlight with no one watching,
at least for long stretches of time.

When I was young I answered an advertisement for custodian of
        the chapel housing the one remaining relic of Saint Cynthia
        Humber,
her arm,
sheathed in hammered silver, resting on a faded green pillow in a
    cloudy glass case.

Now my family has left this out-of-the-way shrine for various
     cities,
but I stay on, too old to abandon the saint's remains, to which I
     have devoted my life
and which only two or three people a year come to visit—secretive
     scholars or addled Americans—
"Saint *Cynthia* Humber," I say, "not a baseball pitcher. She was
     martyred by the Granites of north-east Quebec, descendants
     of those who broiled Saint Lawrence on a grill."
One grizzled man knelt for a breathless hour close to the case, then,
     leaving, changed his expression and said, "There's nothing
     inside the silver, is there."
And I winked and said, "Of course not." Easing his jealousy. And
     mine.
Why would I tell him she reaches down sweet as lobster flesh out of
     the thorny morning sun and touches my lips to waken me
or that she loves to burrow inside my pajama leg like a young cat?

Always between sleeping and waking. Like almost heard singing.

FROM BLOMIDON HEAD

My mind goes into Pearl Island
which lies in the sea without any tension,
a hazed grey body displaying every grain of itself to the grey sky,
the same-coloured sea.

I move at the speed
of Pearl Island and will live in it ten thousand
years after all that we know is forgotten.
Pearl Island is long and hump-backed.

Thirty fathom, master, latitude forty-nine degrees,
eleven minutes and forty seconds, one cable west of Hag
Rock, and thirty more shillings, and when this is done,
an advancement,
bloody cold wind for the time of year, but the king
must know what is in his coffers, tally
the islands,
the miles of coast.

June

23

Benoit's
Cove

Bib
Shadow

Faun
Shadow

today a calm, thinking of Joseph Banks I fished
out the open car window with my eyes and at once
just west of Benoit's Cove caught (1) a Bib Shadow,
Umbra fimbriata, which spilled from the foot of a
poplar stump on uneven ground, it had somewhat
the form of a cast-aside skirt or slip, dark indigo
among dandelions and new grass, also (2) a Faun
Shadow, *Umbra variata*, occurring where an aspen
tree's leaves sifted the falling sunlight into a school
of ovals, soft yellows and greens swimming on a
blistered blue clapboard wall, the whole aggregation
fading and reappearing now and then as though
frightened into some refuge by (3) *Umbra nebulosa*,
shadows of clouds cruising overhead

Dismem-
berment

My blood was up finding such varied species close
together, yet underneath I had the persistent faint
sensation of being nothing more than a ribcage,
flayed eviscerated, like that of a sheep hanging at the
butcher's, the sea air, the odours of buds and pollens
pulled through my chest cavity by the working ribs.
Perhaps with what I collect I hope to flesh myself
out, reconstruct my anatomy in a form less human,
less estranged. Or is it characteristic of the creatures
I search for to erode or digest their observers? If so,
I should list my sense of dismemberment as one
of their properties.

Cobblies

sighted also 2 examples of what the local people call
Cobblies, *Phantasma lascivum,* one (4), probably a Bell
Sprite [*Phantasma medusum* (S.)], flashing in the
corner of my right eye between the blue house and
the road, domed and transparent with his edges
pink-tinted and a little fringed, or so it appeared in
passing—whether an effect of light reflected off the
waves of Humber Arm distorted in the heated air
along the road or some as yet unstudied life form
lacking material substance, I know not—the other
(5), *Phantasma voluptum,* is in the form of an infinite
series of naked female legs high-kicking above the
footlights of a stage, this occurring in my
imagination upon seeing a row of white birch trunks,
Betula papyrifera, diminishing down the grassy slope
to the northwest

24

Aquatic
Faun

today being also fine I was at the mouth of Blomidon
Brook early and took what I hope will prove a complete
aquatic variant of No. (2) [*Umbra salvelinalis
fontinalis* (S.)], this, having mobile crescents of light
in opposed pairs like wings fluttering in abundance,
resided under two feet of clear estuary water on a bed
of ridged sand

in the background, car noise swelled and tapered
on the road from time to time, the tires drumming
hugely on the concrete bridge, and in the intervals
when stillness gathered to a heaviness that had to
drop, a white-throated sparrow would sing very loud
nearby, all of earth's gravity in its words—so good to
have weight, to be drawn in

26

Geological
truancy

yesterday and today low concourse of cloud
obscuring the tops of the Blomidons, no doubt
the rock outcrops and shrubby knolls are dissolved
and widely dispersed in the intense mist, an
absorption of elements I am convinced the rocks
respond to freely, ranging far in a blind
conversation of touch

Rain

loose herds of rain mammoths, shag-sided the colour
of rough-hatchelled tow, blunder out of the northwest
very cold, thrash through the spruce and alders
knocking branches to either side, not a fit day for
venturing out

Carmine Starnino, Editor
Michael Harris, Founding Editor

THE SIGNAL ANTHOLOGY Edited by Michael Harris
MURMUR OF THE STARS: SELECTED SHORTER POEMS Peter Dale Scott
WHAT DANTE DID WITH LOSS Jan Conn
MORNING WATCH John Reibetanz
JOY IS NOT MY PROFESSION Muhammad al-Maghut
   (Translated by John Asfour and Alison Burch)
WRESTLING WITH ANGELS: SELECTED POEMS Doug Beardsley
HIDE & SEEK Susan Glickman
MAPPING THE CHAOS Rhea Tregebov
FIRE NEVER SLEEPS Carla Hartsfield
THE RHINO GATE POEMS George Ellenbogen
SHADOW CABINET Richard Sanger
MAP OF DREAMS Ricardo Sternberg
THE NEW WORLD Carmine Starnino
THE LONG COLD GREEN EVENINGS OF SPRING Elisabeth Harvor
FAULT LINE Laura Lush
WHITE STONE: THE ALICE POEMS Stephanie Bolster
KEEP IT ALL Yves Boisvert (Translated by Judith Cowan)
THE GREEN ALEMBIC Louise Fabiani
THE ISLAND IN WINTER Terence Young
A TINKERS' PICNIC Peter Richardson
SARACEN ISLAND: THE POEMS OF ANDREAS KARAVIS David Solway
BEAUTIES ON MAD RIVER: SELECTED AND NEW POEMS Jan Conn
WIND AND ROOT Brent MacLaine
HISTORIES Andrew Steinmetz
ARABY Eric Ormsby
WORDS THAT WALK IN THE NIGHT Pierre Morency
   (Translated by Lissa Cowan and René Brisebois)
A PICNIC ON ICE: SELECTED POEMS Matthew Sweeney
HELIX: NEW AND SELECTED POEMS John Steffler
HERESIES: THE COMPLETE POEMS OF ANNE WILKINSON, 1924-1961
   Edited by Dean Irvine
CALLING HOME Richard Sanger
FIELDER'S CHOICE Elise Partridge

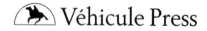 Véhicule Press

www.vehiculepress.com